The children went to the zoo.

They looked at the giraffes.

The giraffes were tall.

They looked at the seals.

The seals were hungry.

They looked at the crocodiles.

The crocodiles were asleep.

They looked at the parrots.

The parrots were noisy.

They looked at the elephants.

The elephants were big.

They looked at the monkeys.

The monkeys were funny.

They looked for Kipper.

RHESUS MONKEYS

Kipper looked like a monkey.